Raising happy and healthy children with diabetes

A GUIDE FOR PARENTS AND DELICIOUS RECIPES

FOR YOUR CHILD AND THE WHOLE FAMILY

BY ELIZABETH AMBROSE

FIRST EDITION 2014

DEDICATION

I dedicate this book to my beautiful God daughter "Nadia", who was diagnosed with Type 1 diabetes at the age of 4 years old.

I also dedicate this book to her parents, for their strength, love and commitment in raising a happy, healthy and confident child.

INTRODUCTION

Every day 70,000 children are diagnosed with diabetes around the world, according to the International Diabetes Federation. In 2013, there were 382 million people with diabetes in the world and it is expected to reach 592 million by 2035.

There are three main types of diabetes: Type 1 diabetes, Type 2 diabetes and Gestational diabetes.

Diabetes Type 1 (formerly known as juvenile diabetes) affects children and young adults. There are 10-15 percent of people affected with this type. It is not know why or how the disease is contracted as more than 80 percent of those diagnosed with the disease have no family history.

The most important aspect about this disease is "management" of the blood sugar levels.

Children diagnosed with this disease can have a normal, happy and healthy life, as long as they have a diabetes management plan that includes exercise, healthy eating and weight control.

Children with diabetes do not have to eat special meals, but they do need to have a meal plan designed specifically for them.

This book is designed to provide parents with a guide and delicious recipes to ensure that your child can have a healthy and happy life.

DISCLAIMER

All rights Reserved:

No part of this publication or the information in it may be quoted from or reproduced in any form by means such as printing, scanning, photocopying or otherwise without prior written permission of the copyright holder.

Disclaimer and Terms of Use:

Effort has been made to ensure that the information in this book is accurate and complete, however, the author and the publisher do not warrant the accuracy of the information, text and graphics contained within the book due to the rapidly changing nature of science, research, known and unknown facts and internet. The Author and the publisher do not hold any responsibility for errors, omissions or contrary interpretation of the subject matter herein. This book is presented solely for motivational and informational purposes only.

First Edition 2014

Copyright © 2014

Table of Contents

DEDICATION 2

INTRODUCTION 3

DISCLAIMER 4

WHAT IS DIABETES TYPE 1 8

SYMPTOMS 9

LIVING WITH DIABETES 10

    Self-management: 10

    A health care team: 10

    Information and support 10

KEEPING TRACK OF BLOOD SUGAR 12

INSULIN 13

COMPLICATIONS 14

SIGNS OF TROUBLE 15

    Low blood sugar (Hypoglycemia): 15

    High blood sugar (Hyperglycemia): 15

DIABETES SELF MANAGEMENT 16

EXERCISING 17

GOING TO SCHOOL 18

EATING HEALTHY GUIDELINE 19

    Carbohydrates 19

    Glycemic Index (GI): 19

    Sugar intake: 19

    Fat consumption 19

    Protein consumption: 20

MEAL PLANS 21

    Types of meal plans 21

    Food labels 21

    Keeping records 21

BREAKFAST RECIPES 22

    Oats and berries parfait 23

    Mixed berry pancake 24

    Quinoa with mixed berries 25

    Omelets with spinach 26

Oatmeal with pumpkin puree	27
Egg muffins	28
Porridge with apricot puree	29
SNACK RECIPES	**30**
Healthy berry salad with red grapes	31
Apricot bar	32
Chocolate chip cookies (low carb-low sugar)	34
Apple and honey scones	35
Creamed rice	37
Spinach and ham English muffin pizzas	38
Baked vegetable chips with yoghurt dip	39
LUNCH RECIPES	**40**
Egg baked with spinach and ham	41
Turkey and avocado salad with toasted seeds	42
Poached eggs with lentils and rocket leaves	43
Pasta salad with pastrami, mushroom and cucumber	44
Pumpkin, potato and leek soup	45
Chicken salad with fruit and vegetables	46
Eggs burrito with black beans	47
DINNER RECIPES	**48**
Lamb with braised lentils	49
Grilled duck with plum and potatoes	50
Asian-marinated salmon with stir-fried noodle	52
Wholemeal fettuccine with broccoli	53
Potato and beef moussaka	54
Picadillo soft taco	55
Baked falafel	56
DESSERTS RECIPES	**58**
Blueberry torte dessert	59
Angel pecan cupcakes	60
Chocolate cake	61
Banana chocolate parfaits	62
Baked cinnamon stuffed apples	63
Mini pumpkins tarts	64

- Frozen strawberries fruit pops 65
- DRINK RECIPES 66
  - Celery Smoothie 67
  - Blueberry Orange Frappe 68
  - Cranberry Milkshake 69
  - Acai Banana Smoothie 70
  - Mango and Pineapple Frappe 71
  - Kale and Apple Smoothie 72
  - Sugar free hot chocolate 73
- REFERENCE 74
- CONCLUSION 75

WHAT IS DIABETES TYPE 1

Diabetes is a disease that causes your body either being unable to produce insulin or produce insulin but does not work properly, still raising sugar levels too high.

Diabetes Type 1, is when the pancreas (a flat gland that helps digest food) cannot make a "hormone" called insulin. Your body stills produces glucose (the sugar used as fuel in your body), but it does not go into your body cells to give you energy. The glucose, instead, stays in your blood and causes your blood sugar levels to get very high making you sick.

Diabetes Type 2, is when the pancreas produces insulin, but it does not work properly, hence raising blood sugar levels.

SYMPTOMS

When the sugar levels are very high your body produces the following symptom:

- Feeling very tired
- Feeling thirsty
- Losing weight
- Wanting to pass lots of urine
- Feeling hungry
- Not feeling well in general

When Type 1 diabetes is not diagnosed early enough, a more serious condition can develop known as Diabetic Ketoacidosis (DKA). This condition requires urgent medical attention. The symptoms are:

- Nausea
- Vomiting
- Abdominal pain
- Drowsiness
- Rapid, deep breathing

LIVING WITH DIABETES

Diabetes is a condition that requires self-management, support and continuous review.

A person with diabetes needs:

Self-management:
- Eating healthy foods
- Exercising
- Taking medication and /or insulin
- Monitoring your blood sugar levels
- Taking care with oral hygiene and foot care.

A health care team:
A diabetes educator is a registered nurse that cares for and teaches people with diabetes. They monitor your progress and keep you informed about all the aspects about diabetes, such as:

- Monitoring your glucose levels
- Taking insulin
- Traveling safety tips
- Managing diabetes when you are sick

An accredited practicing dietitian provides you with individual and practical advice about nutrition. They can provide you with a meal plan to help you with:

- Controlling your triglycerides and cholesterol
- Manage glucose levels
- Keeping a healthy body weight

An exercise physiotherapist or physiologist, to provide you advice with exercise and activities.

You also need: an endocrinologist, medical eye specialist or optometrist and podiatrist.

Information and support
Many people with diabetes find it helpful to be able to share with other people their experience.

You can ask your doctor, contact your local community for more information or visit the following sites:

Location	Website
International	www.idf.org
	www.novonordisk.com
	www.epodiatry.com
	www.type1diabetes.about.com
America	www.diabetes.org
UK	www.diabetes.co.uk
Australia	www.diabetesaustralia.com.au
Canada	www.diabetes.ca
France	www.afd.asso.fr
Italy	www.siditalia.it
Spain	www.sediabetes.org
Mexico	www.fmdiabetes.com
Brazil	www.diabetes.org.br

KEEPING TRACK OF BLOOD SUGAR

You may need to keep an eye on your child's blood sugar several times a day, but at least four times a day depending on what type of insulin therapy your child has been prescribed.

Testing is absolutely necessary to ensure that your child's blood sugar is within his/her target.

You or your doctor may keep records of the blood glucose readings, depending on whether you are using the method of frequent finger prickling or a blood glucose meter.

Continuous glucose monitoring (CGM) is one of the newest methods to monitor blood sugar levels, but is generally used by people who have developed hypoglycemia unawareness.

INSULIN

Children and young adults diagnosed with Type 1 diabetes requires insulin in order to survive. Your doctor may prescribe a combination of these types, depending on the child's needs and age.

There are many types, and includes:

Rapid-acting insulin (starts acting after 5-15 minutes, peaks in 1 hour),

Short-acting insulin (starts working after about 30 minute, peaks in 2hours),

Long-acting insulin (no peak, has a coverage of 20-26 hours) and

Intermediate-acting insulin (starts working after about 30 minute, peaks in 4-6 hours)

Insulin can be injected with a fine needle or pen; you can also use a pump.

COMPLICATIONS

Monitoring and keeping your child's blood sugar levels on track reduces the risk of complications, however sometimes Type 1 diabetes could affect your child's heart, nerves, kidney and eyes. Long term complication may develop gradually and can be life threatening.

Type 1 diabetes might cause the following complications, over long period of time or later in life:

Heart and blood vessel disease: including heart attack, stroke, and high blood pressure.

Nerve damage (neuropathy): especially in the legs, causing numbness, burning, tingling or pain.

Kidney damage (nephropathy): damage of the blood vessel can cause kidney failure or irreversible kidney disease.

Eye damage: can cause damage to the retina (retinopathy). Retinopathy can cause blindness. Diabetes can also cause cataracts and risk of glaucoma.

Foot damage: Poor blood flow and nerve damage can cause serious foot complications.

Skin conditions: diabetes can cause bacterial infection, fungal infection and itching.

Osteoporosis: bone mineral density might be lower than normal in people with diabetes, increasing risk of osteoporosis as an adult.

SIGNS OF TROUBLE

Some short-term complication can arise despite all effort to manage the condition. These complications can cause seizures and loss of consciousness.

Low blood sugar (Hypoglycemia): when the blood sugar levels drops below the child's target. Drop in sugar levels can be caused by skipping meals, too much insulin injected or too much physical activities. Early symptoms include: sweating, drowsiness, hunger, headaches, confusion, change of behavior, irritability and loss of consciousness.

If the blood sugar reading is low, give your child a source of sugar such as, fruit juice, regular soda, hard candy or glucose tablet. Re-test in 15 minutes, and if still not normal, give your child more sugar and re-test again in 15 minutes. Repeat until the reading is normal.

Ensure that your child always carries some type of sugar supply with her/him, as well as, a glucagon emergency kit (at home, school and any outings).

High blood sugar (Hyperglycemia): when the blood sugar levels rises above your child's target. Rise can be caused by eating too much, not enough insulin, eating the wrong foods or illness. Symptoms includes: increase thirst, blurred vision, dry mouth, fatigue, recurrent urination, nausea and yeast infection (in infants and toddlers).

If the blood sugar level is high, administer a correction insulin shot. Re-test sugar levels after 15 minutes. Check with your doctor if your child needs a change in the meals plans or medication. If the sugar reading is above 250mg/dL (13.9mmol/L) ask your doctor to check for ketones. Ensure that the child does not exercise. If blood sugar is above 300 mg/dL (16.mmol/L) seek emergency care. Increase ketones in your child's urine might be a sign of diabetic ketoacidosis (DKA).

DIABETES SELF MANAGEMENT

When a child is diagnosed at early age with diabetes, parents are very involved in their child's management of diabetes. It is important, however, as the child grows older, that they can become confident in managing their diabetes independently.

In order for your child to develop the skills and confidence, you are required to:

- Involve your child in their diabetes management from the beginning, in accordance with their age.
- Make certain that your child understands that they are not alone and that it is not their sole responsibility.
- Encourage your child to attend diabetes camps.
- Help your child to develop lifelong skills and confidence.
- As they grow older and independent, encourage your child to schedule their own appointments with their health plan team.

EXERCISING

Children diagnosed with Type 1 diabetes needs to have a healthy diet and exercise regularly. The child needs 30 minutes of moderate exercise most days in order to: lower blood sugar levels, lower cholesterol, and lower blood pressure, reduce stress and anxiety, increase self-esteem, increase muscle and bone strength and enhance the quality of sleep.

The child needs a combination of exercises:

Exercise to strengthen the heart: such as aerobics, swimming, basketball, jogging, hockey, jumping, biking, cross country, etc.

Exercise to strengthen the muscles: push-ups, pull ups, rowing, bike riding running, skating, etc.

Exercise that increase flexibility: dancing, yoga, martial arts, gymnastics, stretches, etc.

Exercise to keep balance: In order to maintain your weight or wanting to lose weight.

Exercise to feel happier: when you exercise you release endorphins, which makes you feel happy. Having a strong body and being able to do all kinds of activities makes you feel good about yourself.

GOING TO SCHOOL

When your child is diagnosed with diabetes, it is natural to feel concerned about your child commencing or returning to school. As a parent, it is your responsibility to provide all the information required to ensure that the school supports your child with his/hers diabetes management during school time.

The must be provided the following information to the school:

- Management plan during school hours: including exercise, dietary needs and insulin regimes.
- Management plan for hypoglycemia and hyperglycemia.
- Emergency contacts
- Communication book to inform of diabetes related issues.
- Management plan for excursions and camps.
- Provide information about symptoms of complications with diabetes.
- Encourage your child to explain to his/her friends about his/her condition.

EATING HEALTHY GUIDELINE

Eating healthy when you have diabetes, has many benefits and includes: maintaining a healthy blood sugar level, healthy body weight, blood pressure, reach target blood lipid levels and prevent or slow diabetes complications.

A simple eating plan includes:

More	Less
Eating regular meals.	Avoid lollies and chocolates.
Eating reduced serving size.	Avoid sweet drinks (soft drinks, cordials, flavored waters and energy drinks.
Include a small serving of high fibre carbohydrate at each meal.	Don't add salt when cooking. Reduce high salt foods.
Eating reduced fat or low fat dairy products.	Cakes and baked items should be consumed occasionally.
Eating lean meats, eggs, legumes, vegetables, fruits, tofu and nuts.	Limit unhealthy saturated fats found in full cream milk, ice cream, yoghurt, butter and cheese.
Include some healthy saturated fats such as avocado, seeds and nuts, olive, canola and sunflower oil.	
Include fish in your diet at least 2-3 times a week such as salmon, sardines and tuna.	

Carbohydrates: is the best source of energy and has the greatest effect on blood sugar levels.

By spreading your carbohydrates evenly on each meal, it will help you to maintain good energy levels and glucose levels in your blood.

If you take insulin, it is a good idea to eat snacks in between meals.

Glycemic Index (GI): You should aim at eating foods that are low in glycemic index (produces a slower rise in blood glucose levels), at least one per meal. Includes carbohydrates such as high fibre breads, cereals (grainy and oats), pasta and low GI rice, quinoa, legumes, most fruits, and low fat dairy products.

Sugar intake: You can include small amount of sugar in your diet, however, it should be included in nutritional foods, such as; high fibre breakfast with dried fruit, canned fruit in natural juice or low-fat dairy products.

Fat consumption: try to eat less saturated fat such as meat fat, cream, butter, palm and coconut oil, full fat dairy products which increase your chances of heart disease and weight gain. Choose polyunsaturated fats and oils such as corn, sesame, sunflower, fish, nuts and seeds. Also include monounsaturated fats such as canola and olive oil, avocados, nuts and seeds.

Protein consumption: Your body needs protein to repair and grow. Generally proteins do not affect your blood sugar levels. Includes lean meats, skinless poultry, soy, seafood, egg, unsalted nuts and legumes (these also include carbohydrates, so might affect your glucose levels).

MEAL PLANS

You diabetes team or dietitian will provide you with a meal plan, according to your age. Meal plans generally include which food groups to select and when you should eat, but it does not tell you what foods to eat.

Types of meal plans
There are three types of meal plans:

Constant carbohydrate meal plans: you need to include a specific amount of carbohydrates in each meal and snack, followed by insulin. This shall be at the same times and similar doses.

Carbohydrate counting: where the amount of carbohydrate consumed matches the insulin doses. You need to count the carbohydrate grams being consumed.

Exchange meal plan: This plan focuses on carbohydrates, proteins and fats being consumed. There are six groups in this type of plan: fruit, vegetables, meat, starch and fat. You need to eat certain amount from each group based on the amount of calories a particular person needs.

Food labels
Food labels are very informative, as they provide you with nutritional facts such as: calories, carbohydrates and protein, fat and sodium amounts per serving. This information helps you to keep track of your blood sugar.

Keeping records
When you are on a meal plan, make sure to keep records.

Records include: what you eat, your blood sugar levels, carbohydrates or meal exchange consumed.

BREAKFAST RECIPES

Oats and berries parfait

Ingredients:

- 8oz. (225g) nonfat or low fat plain Greek yoghurt
- 1 cup fresh blueberries and strawberries
- ½ cup oats (quick cooking)
- Fresh honey or maple syrup

Method:

- In a dessert bowl, place ½ cup of fruit.
- Add low fat yoghurt
- Add a layer of oats with honey
- Add the remaining fruit
- Serve

Nutritional facts:

Serves: 2
Calories: 110 Cal
Fats: 1.3 g
Carbohydrates: 22.3 g
Fiber: 2.1 g
Sugars: 8.2 g
Protein: 2.7 g

Mixed berry pancake

Ingredients:

- 1 egg
- ½ tablespoon butter, softened
- 1 cup low fat milk
- 1 cup whole wheat flour
- ½ teaspoon sea salt
- 2 teaspoons baking powder
- 1 teaspoon sugar
- 2 tablespoons vegetable oil
- ½ cup fresh mixed berries

Method:

- In a large bowl, add egg and beat until light.
- Add in butter and beat again.
- Add milk, stir and set aside.
- In another bowl, combine flour, sea salt, baking powder and sugar and mix.
- Gradually add into the egg mixture and mix until well combined.
- Grease a non-stick frying pan with vegetable oil.
- Pour ¼ cup (approximately) of the mixture into the pan.
- Cook for 2-3 minutes and flip.
- Cook for 2 minutes from the other side.
- Remove to a serving plate and top with mixed berries.
- Make pancakes from the remaining batter following the same procedure and serve.

Nutritional facts:

Serves: 12
Calories: 81 Cal
Fats: 3.4g
Carbohydrates: 10.4g
Dietary Fiber: 0.5g
Sugars: 1.9g
Protein: 2.3g

Quinoa with mixed berries

Ingredients:

- 1½ cups quinoa
- ¾ cup almond milk, unsweetened
- ¾ cup mixed dried berries
- 1½ tablespoons maple syrup
- 1 teaspoon vanilla extract
- ½ teaspoon ground cinnamon

Method:

- Place the quinoa in a saucepan and add water to cover.
- Heat until quinoa is well cooked.
- Remove from the heat and allow it to cool.
- Drain and place into a bowl.
- Add in almond milk and dried berries.
- Mix in maple syrup, vanilla extract and cinnamon.
- Divide into 6 bowls and serve.

Nutritional facts:

Serves: 6
Calories: 242 Cal
Fats: 9.7g
Carbohydrates: 33.0g
Fiber: 4.2g
Sugars: 5.3g
Protein: 6.5g

Omelets with spinach

Ingredients:

- 3 eggs, beaten
- 1 tablespoon extra-virgin olive oil
- 1 cup spinach leaves, chopped
- 1 teaspoon fresh basil, finely chopped
- 1 avocado, sliced
- Freshly ground pepper to taste

Method:

- In a pan, heat oil at medium heat and add beaten eggs.
- When eggs are almost set, add spinach on one half of the omelet.
- Sprinkle with basil and pepper.
- Fold in half and reduce heat.
- Cover and simmer for 1 minute.
- Serve with avocados slices on the side.

Nutritional Facts:

Serves: 2
Calories: 363 Cal
Fat: 33.2g
Carbohydrate: 9.7 g
Fiber: 1.7 g
Sugar: 2.2 g
Protein: 10.7 g

Oatmeal with pumpkin puree

Ingredients:

- 1 cup dry oats, cooked
- ½ cup pumpkin, puree
- 1 teaspoon pumpkin spice, not sugar
- 4 eggs whites (optional)
- ¼ cup pecans (per serving)
- Maple syrup to taste

Method:

- In a pot, boil pumpkin, drain and puree. Set aside to cool.
- Prepare oats in accordance to the instructions on the packet.
- Just before oats are fully cooked, add eggs whites.
- Stir briskly until all is combined and smooth.
- Add pumpkin puree and spice and stir.
- Serve in a breakfast bowl.
- Sprinkle with pecans and add syrup.

Nutritional facts:

Serves: 4
Calories: 204 Cal
Fat: 7g
Carbohydrate: 31 g
Fiber: 4 g
Sugar: 14 g
Protein: 7 g

Egg muffins

Ingredients:

- 4 eggs
- 2 egg whites
- 1 tablespoon low fat milk
- ¼ to ½ cup grated cheddar cheese
- ½ cup broccoli florets
- Salt and pepper to taste
- Spray oil

Method:

- Pre-heat oven at 180 deg. F (350 deg. C).
- Steam broccoli and chop.
- In a bowl, add egg, egg whites and milk and beat.
- Add salt and pepper to taste.
- Add cheese and mix.
- Add broccoli and mix again.
- In a muffin tray, greased with spray oil, add egg mixture to ¾ full.
- Top with grated cheese.
- Cook for 20-25 minutes.

Nutritional facts:

Serves: 6
Calories: 51 Cal
Fat: 3.0 g
Carbohydrate: 0.9 g
Fiber: 0.0 g
Sugar: 0.6 g
Protein: 5.2 g

Porridge with apricot puree

Ingredients:

- 6 oz. (175 g) rolled oats
- 3 cups (750 ml) skimmed milk or water
- 2 teaspoons brown sugar
- 7 oz. (200g) fresh apricots, poached
- 1 ¼ cup fresh orange juice

Method:

- In a pot with water poach apricots and simmer for 10 minutes.
- Drain apricots.
- In the same pot, with the apricots add orange juice and bring to the boil again.
- Simmer for another 10 minutes.
- In the meantime, in another pot with milk (or water), add sugar and oats.
- Bring to the boil and simmer for 10 minutes.
- In a blender add apricot and pulse until smooth.
- Place porridge in a bowl and top with apricot puree.

Nutritional facts:

Serves: 4
Calories: 283 Cal
Fat: 3.1g
Carbohydrate: 52.2 g
Fiber: 5.4 g
Sugar: 13.0 g
Protein: 11.8 g

SNACK RECIPES

Healthy berry salad with red grapes

Ingredients:

- ½ cup strawberries, halved
- ½ cup blueberries
- ½ cup raspberries
- 1 cup red grapes, halved
- 1 orange, peeled and sectioned
- 1 tablespoon lime juice
- 1 tablespoon lime zest
- 2 tablespoons pomegranate seeds

Method:

- Add strawberries, blueberries, raspberries, red grapes and the sectioned orange in a large bowl.
- Add in lime juice, lime zest and pomegranate seeds and toss well.
- Place in the refrigerator.
- Serve chilled.

Nutritional facts:

Serves: 4
Calories: 52 Cal
Fats: 0.3g
Carbohydrates: 13.0g
Fiber: 4.1g
Sugars: 8.4g
Protein: 1.0g

Apricot bar

Ingredients:

- ¾ cup dried apricots, split
- 1/3 cup water
- ¾ cup all purpose flour
- 1 teaspoon baking powder
- ¾ teaspoon cinnamon
- ¼ teaspoon baking soda
- 1 egg
- ½ cup granulated sugar
- 1 tablespoon canola oil
- 1 tablespoon grated lemon zest
- 1 teaspoon vanilla
- 2 tablespoons powdered sugar

Method:

- Pre-heat oven to 350 deg. F (180 deg. C)
- In a pan, add water, half of the apricots and simmer for 2 minutes (covered).
- Allow to cool. Do not drain.
- In a blender, puree the cooled apricots for 1 minute.
- Add sugar, oil, egg, zest and vanilla and blend for 30 seconds.
- Chop the remaining apricots.
- In a bowl, add flour, cinnamon, baking powder and baking soda and whisk.
- Add the chopped apricots and mix.
- Add the puree apricots and stir until all is blended together.
- In a greased baking tray, add the mixture and distribute uniformly.
- Cook for 18-20 minutes until golden brown.
- Remove from the oven and dust with powdered sugar.
- Allow to cool before cutting.

Nutritional facts:

Serves: 20
Calories: 16 Cal
Fats: 0.9 g
Carbohydrates: 1.8 g
Fiber: 0.0 g
Sugars: 1.4 g

Protein: 0.4 g

Chocolate chip cookies (low carb-low sugar)

Ingredients:

- 1/3 cup butter, softened
- 1 egg
- 1 teaspoon vanilla
- 1/3 cup granulated sugar
- 1/3 cup light brown sugar, firmly packed
- ¾ cup all purpose flour
- ½ teaspoon baking soda
- ¼ teaspoon salt
- ½ semi-sweet chocolate chips or mini chocolate chips

Method:

- In a bowl, add butter, vanilla, sugars and egg and beat with electric mixer.
- In another bowl, mix flour, salt and baking soda.
- Add to the butter mix and stir until all combined.
- Add chocolate chips and stir.
- Pre-heat oven at 350 deg. F. (180 deg. C).
- In a baking tray lined with baking paper, place rounded teaspoons of the batter.
- Cook for 10 minutes until golden brown.
- Remove from tray and cool cookies on a wire rack.

Nutritional facts:

Serves: 16
Calories: 4.2 Cal
Fats: 4.2 g
Carbohydrates: 11.6 g
Fiber: 0.0 g
Sugars: 7.2 g
Protein: 1.0 g

Apple and honey scones

Ingredients:

- 2 cups all purpose flour
- ¼ teaspoon salt
- ¼ teaspoon baking soda
- ¼ teaspoon ground nutmeg
- 2 teaspoons baking powder
- 1 ¼ teaspoon ground cinnamon
- 1 -2/3 cup wheat germ, toasted
- 1/3 cup margarine
- 1 ¼ cups apple, cored, peeled and finely chopped
- ½ cup skim milk
- ¼ cup honey
- 1 tablespoon sugar

Method:

- Pre-heat oven at 400 deg. F (200 deg. C)
- In a bowl, add 2/3 cup wheat germ, baking soda, flour, baking powder, and salt and mix.
- Add margarine and combine until mixture appears to be fragmented.
- Add milk, honey and apple to make a dough.
- Prepare a surface with flour and place the dough.
- Knead for few minutes, gently.
- With a rolling pin flatten the dough into 9 inch circle.
- In a bowl, add 1 tablespoon sugar, the remaining wheat germ and ¼ teaspoon cinnamon.
- Sprinkle over the dough.
- Cut dough into 10 round pieces.
- Place on a greased baking tray, about ½ -inch apart.
- Cook for 16-18 minutes, until golden brown.

Nutritional facts:

Serves: 10
Calories: 259 Cal
Fats: 8.3 g
Carbohydrates: 39.5 g

Fiber: 4.0 g
Sugars: 11.4g
Protein: 8.6 g

Creamed rice

Ingredients:

- ½ cup long grain rice
- ½ cup water
- 4 cups milk
- ¼ cup sugar
- 1 teaspoon vanilla

Method:

- In a pot, add water and rice and boil.
- Add milk slowly, stir and add sugar.
- Simmer for 30 minutes.
- From time to time, stir to prevent rice sticking to the pan.
- Check if the rice has thickened too much, add more milk if required.
- Add vanilla.

Nutritional facts:

Serves: 4
Calories: 256 Cal
Fats: 5.2 g
Carbohydrates: 43.1g
Fiber: g
Sugars: 23.7 g
Protein: 9.7 g

Spinach and ham English muffin pizzas

Ingredients:

- 2 whole wheat English muffins, cut in half
- 4 tablespoons frozen spinach (chopped), thawed and drained
- 6 tablespoons tomato/garlic sauce (pizza sauce)
- 2 oz. (60g) lower-sodium ham, deli style, chopped
- ½ cup reduced fat mozzarella cheese, shredded

Method:

- Pre-heat oven at 425 deg. F (220 deg. C)
- Add ¼ of the spinach, ¼ of the sauce and ¼ of the ham to each muffin halved.
- Sprinkle shredded mozzarella.
- In a baking tray, lined with baking paper, place each mini pizza.
- Bake for 8 minutes or until cheese is golden brown.

Nutritional facts:

Serves: 4
Calories: 130 Cal
Fats: 3.5 g
Carbohydrates: 17 g
Fiber: 3 g
Sugars: 5 g
Protein: 10 g

Baked vegetable chips with yoghurt dip

Ingredients:

- 1 zucchini, medium size, sliced
- 1 parsnip, medium size, sliced
- 1 potato, medium size , peeled and sliced
- 1 teaspoon salt (optional)
- ½ cup non-fat plain Greek yoghurt
- 1/3 skim milk
- 2 tablespoons of ranch dressing powder mix

Method:

- Pre-heat oven at 200 deg. F (95 deg. C)
- In a baking tray, lined with baking paper and sprayed with oil, add potato slices.
- Top with another baking sheet, add zucchini slices.
- With another layer of baking sheet, add parsnip slices.
- Spray each layer of vegetables with oil and salt.
- Bake for 1 hour.
- Rotate baking sheets until vegetables are crisp.
- Bake for additional 30-60 minutes.
- In the meantime, in a bowl, add milk, ranch dressing powder and yoghurt and mix.
- Refrigerate until vegetables are ready.
- Remove vegetable chips from oven and allow cooling.
- Serve with dip.

Nutritional facts:

Serves: 4
Calories: 90 Cal
Fats: 0.0 g
Carbohydrates: 17 g
Fiber: 2 g
Sugars: 6 g
Protein: 5 g

LUNCH RECIPES

Egg baked with spinach and ham

Ingredients:

- 6oz. (175g) baby spinach leaves
- 1 tablespoon of water
- 4oz. (100g) ham, sliced and chopped
- 1 tomato, cut into 4
- 4 eggs
- 4 tablespoons light crème fraiche
- 1 ½ oz. (40g) mature cheddar cheese, grated
- Salt (optional) and pepper to taste
- Multigrain bread

Method:

- In a pan with water, add spinach and cook until soft for 2-3 minutes.
- In 4 mini pudding basins or molds, add spinach, ham and tomato.
- Crack an egg on each mold.
- Add a tablespoon of crème fraiche on each mold.
- Sprinkle cheese, salt and pepper.
- Pre-heat oven at 400 deg. F (200 deg. C)
- On a baking sheet, place molds and cook for 10 minutes until eggs are cooked.
- Serve with bread.

Nutritional facts:

Serves: 4
Calories: 178 Cal
Fat: 13g
Carbohydrate: 2 g
Fiber: 1.0 g
Sugar: 0.8 g
Protein: 14 g

Turkey and avocado salad with toasted seeds

Ingredients:

- 14 ½ oz. (450g.) cooked turkey, sliced
- 1 avocado, sliced
- 2 red apples, cored and sliced
- 1 punnet mustard cress
- 4 oz. (125g) mixed salad leaves
- 2 oz. (50g) toasted seeds (pumpkin or sunflower)
- 3 tablespoons apple juice
- 3 tablespoons low fat natural yoghurt
- 1 teaspoon honey
- 1 teaspoon wholegrain mustard
- Wholegrain rye bread

Method:

- In a bowl, add turkey, apples, avocado, salad leaves, seeds and mustard cress and mix.
- In another bowl, mix apple juice, yoghurt, mustard and honey.
- Combine together and serve with bread on the side.

Nutritional facts:

Serves: 4
Calories: 372 Cal
Fat: 18 g
Carbohydrate: 15 g
Fiber: 6.7g
Sugar: 18.2g
Protein: 39 g

Poached eggs with lentils and rocket leaves

Ingredients:

- 8oz. (250g) puy lentils
- 1 ¾ cups (450g) vegetable stock
- 1 teaspoon olive oil
- 4 spring onions, finely sliced
- 3 tomatoes, chopped
- 4 oz. (125g) rocket leaves
- 4 eggs
- Salt (optional) and pepper

Method:

- In a pot, add lentils and stock.
- Bring to the boil, reduce heat and simmer for 40 minutes, drain.
- In a pan, add oil and sauté spring onions and tomatoes for 2 minutes.
- Add lentil and rocket and stir.
- Add salt and pepper.
- In a pot, poach eggs, one by one.
- Serve lentils and top with poached eggs.

Nutritional facts:

Serves: 4
Calories: 329 Cal
Fat: 7.5 g
Carbohydrate: 43.6 g
Fiber: 11.3g
Sugar: 5.3 g
Protein: 24.7 g

Pasta salad with pastrami, mushroom and cucumber

Ingredients:

- 7 Oz. (200g) lasagnette (broken into quarters) (you can use other pastas such as spirelli or penne)
- 2 tablespoons red wine vinegar
- ¼ cup olive oil
- ½ teaspoon Dijon mustard
- 1 clove garlic, minced
- 9 oz. (250g) pastrami, cut into strips (from lean beef)
- 1 stalk celery, sliced
- 2 tomatoes, cut in wedges
- 1 Lebanese cucumber , thinly sliced
- 2.8 oz. (80g) button mushrooms, thinly sliced
- ¼ fresh coriander, chopped
- Salt (optional) and fresh grounded pepper to taste

Method:

- In a pot with water (salted), add pasta and cook until dente.
- Drain and place in a salad bowl.
- Add pastrami slices, mushroom, celery, cucumber, tomatoes and mix with the pasta.
- In another bowl, mix vinegar, mustard, garlic, oil, salt and pepper, until all combined.
- Add the oil/vinegar mixture to the pasta salad and toss.
- Cover and refrigerate for several hours.
- Serve and sprinkle with coriander.

Nutritional facts:

Serves: 4
Calories: 415 Cal
Fat: 18.4 g
Carbohydrate: 39.9 g
Fiber: 5.0 g
Sugar: 3.9 g
Protein: 24.1g

Pumpkin, potato and leek soup

Ingredients:

- 1 pumpkin, peeled and cubed
- 2 leeks, white part only, thinly sliced
- 2 potatoes, peeled, cubed
- 1 ½ cups water
- 1 cup of low fat milk
- ½ cup cream
- 1 tablespoon fresh parsley, chopped
- Fresh grated nutmeg to taste
- Salt and white pepper to taste

Method:

- In a pot, add cubed potatoes, pumpkin, leeks and salt.
- Bring to the boil, reduce heat and simmer for 30 minutes.
- In a blender, add vegetables with the liquid and puree.
- Place the puree back to the pot and bring to the boil.
- Simmer for 5 minutes and add milk and stir.
- Reduce heat and simmer for another 2 minutes.
- Add cream, salt, pepper and nutmeg and cook.
- Serve with a sprinkle of parsley.

Nutritional facts:

Serves: 4
Calories: 302 Cal
Fat: 12 g
Carbohydrate: 45 g
Fiber: 6 g
Sugar: 0 g
Protein: 7 g

Chicken salad with fruit and vegetables

Ingredients:

- 1 ½ cups chicken breast, cubed
- 1 cup seedless grapes, halved
- ½ cup pineapple tidbits, drained
- ¼ cup celery, chopped
- 2 tablespoons plain yoghurt
- 2 tablespoons low fat mayonnaise
- 1 ½ cups crisp chow mein noodles
- ½ cup carrots, grated
- 2 tablespoons fresh chive, chopped
- ½ teaspoon salt

Method:

- In a salad bowl, add chicken, celery, pineapple and grapes and mix.
- In another bowl, mix mayonnaise, yoghurt, and salt.
- Tip the mayonnaise/yoghurt mixture on the chicken, mix and cover.
- Refrigerate for 1 hour.
- In the meantime, cook the noodles in accordance with the instructions.
- When ready mix with carrots.
- Divide into 4 servings.
- Top with chicken/vegetables/fruit mixture and sprinkle with chives.

Nutritional facts:

Serves: 4
Calories: 245 Cal
Fat: 9 g
Carbohydrate: 22 g
Fiber: 2 g
Sugar: 0 g
Protein: 21 g

Eggs burrito with black beans

Ingredients:

- 1 cup canned black beans, rinse and drained
- 1/3 cup chunky salsa, bottled.
- 4 eggs
- 2 tablespoons milk
- 1 tomato, thinly sliced
- ½ cup crumbled "queso fresco" cheese or Monterey Jack cheese or light cheddar cheese
- ¼ cup sour cream
- 4 teaspoon fresh mint, chopped
- ¼ black pepper
- Pinch of salt

Method:

- In a pan, over low heat, add beans and mash slightly.
- Add salsa and mix. Cover.
- In a bowl, add milk, eggs, salt and pepper and whisk.
- In another pan, sprayed with oil, add ¼ cup of egg mixture spread evenly over the pan.
- Cook for 1 to 2 minutes until brown on each side.
- Slide onto a plate and add bean mixture.
- Scatter some tomato and cheese.
- Fold into quarters to form burrito.
- Add sour cream and dash of mint.
- Repeat process for the remaining serves.

Nutritional facts:

Serves: 4
Calories: 179 Cal
Fat: 4 g
Carbohydrate: 14 g
Fiber: g
Sugar: 0 g
Protein: 14 g

DINNER RECIPES

Lamb with braised lentils

Ingredients:

- 4 lean lamb steaks
- Juice and grated rind of 1 lemon
- 1 tablespoon rosemary, chopped
- 1 clove garlic, minced
- 2 lean smoked back bacon rashers, chopped
- 2 onions, sliced
- 1 carrot, finely chopped
- 1 celery stick, finely chopped
- 8 oz. (250g) green or puy lentils
- 1 ¾ cups (450ml) vegetable stock

Method:

- In a bowl add, lemon juice and rind, garlic and rosemary and mix.
- Brush steaks with the mixture.
- In a nonstick pan, at high heat, add steaks.
- Cook for 1 minute on each side (or to your liking).
- Remove steaks and set aside.
- In the same pan, add onions, bacon, celery and carrot.
- Fry for 2-3 minutes until soft.
- Add lentils, stock and the lamb steaks
- Bring to the boil, reduce heat and simmer for 30-40 minutes.
- When the lentils are soft and stock is absorbed, serve.

Nutritional facts:

Serves: 4
Calories: 492 Cal
Fat: 17 g
Carbohydrate: 38 g
Fiber: 11.0 g
Sugar: 2.7 g
Protein: 55.4 g

Grilled duck with plum and potatoes

Ingredients:

- 14 ½ oz. (450g) potatoes, washed and sliced
- 2 cloves garlic, minced
- 1 teaspoon thyme, chopped
- 2 tablespoons olive oil
- ½ cup water
- 4 boneless duck breast, skinned
- 4 teaspoons Chinese five-spice powder
- 2 onions, sliced
- 1 tablespoon sugar
- 2 tablespoons white wine vinegar
- 6 plums, stoned, halved and sliced
- Pepper to taste
- Salt to taste
- Steamed green vegetables

Method:

- Pre-heat oven at 350deg. F (180 deg. C).
- Mix water and 1 tablespoon of oil.
- In a baking dish, add potatoes, thyme and garlic.
- Add water/oil mixture, salt and pepper and cover with foil.
- Cook for 1 hour until potatoes are soft.
- In the meantime, brush duck with the five-spice powder.
- Cook duck on the grill or pan for 3-4 minutes on each side.
- In a small pan, heat the remaining tablespoon of oil.
- Add onion and sugar and sauté for 10 minutes.
- Add plum, vinegar, salt and pepper.
- Cook for further 10 minutes.
- Remove duck from the grill and slice.
- Serve with potatoes, plum and vegetables.

Nutritional facts:

Serves: 4
Calories: 375 Cal
Fat: 12 g
Carbohydrate: 39 g
Fiber: 5.4 g

Sugar: 16.5 g
Protein: 38.0 g

Asian-marinated salmon with stir-fried noodle

Ingredients:

- 4 oz. (125g) x 4 pieces of salmon (each)
- 1 clove garlic, minced
- 2 tablespoons soy sauce
- 1 inch (2.5 cm) piece fresh ginger, peeled and grated
- 2 tablespoons rice wine vinegar
- 1 tablespoon sesame oil
- 8oz. (250g) medium rice noodles
- 7 oz. (200g) mangetout, halved lengthways
- 5 oz. (150g) shiitakes mushrooms, trimmed and sliced
- 4 spring onions, sliced
- 3 ½ oz. (100g) bean sprouts
- 2 pak choi, cut in 4 lengthways

Method:

- In a bowl, add ginger, garlic, vinegar, soy sauce, and ½ tablespoon oil and mix.
- In a shallow dish, place salmon and marinate with the mixture.
- Cover and set aside for 10 minutes.
- In the grill or a nonstick frying pan, cook the salmon for 2-3 minutes.
- Keep the marinade.
- In the meantime, prepare the noodles in accordance with instructions.
- In a pan, add the other ½ tablespoons of oil and heat.
- Place mushroom, mangetout, bean sprouts, spring onions, pack choi and stir for 3- 4 minutes.
- Add marinade and noodles.
- Mix well and heat.
- Remove from pan, serve with salmon.

Nutritional facts:

Serves: 4
Calories: 528 Cal
Fat: 18 g
Carbohydrate: 58 g
Fiber: 4.9 g
Sugar: 7.5 g
Protein: 34.6 g

Wholemeal fettuccine with broccoli

Ingredients:

- 14 oz. (400g) wholemeal fettuccine
- 25 oz. (700g) broccoli (small florets)
- ½ cup olive oil
- 2 cloves garlic, minced
- 21 oz. (600g) tomatoes, skinned, seeded and chopped
- 1 tablespoon toasted pine nuts
- 1 tablespoon fresh parsley, chopped
- Cooking salt

Method:

- In a pot, add broccoli and salt.
- Cook for 3-4 minutes until soft-crisp.
- Remove broccoli and place under cold water quickly and set aside.
- In the same pot with boiling water, add fetuccine and cook until al dente.
- In the meantime, in a pan, add oil, and garlic and sauté.
- Add tomatoes and simmer for 5 minutes.
- Add pine nuts and mix.
- Add broccoli and parsley and mix again.
- Drain pasta and serve with broccoli mix.

Nutritional facts:

Serves: 6
Calories: 304 Cal
Fat: 19.6 g
Carbohydrate: 63.8 g
Fiber: 11.5 g
Sugar: 6.9 g
Protein: 12.7 g

Potato and beef moussaka

Ingredients:

- 2 pounds (900g) potatoes, sliced into ¼ inch thick
- 1 cup onion, chopped
- 2 cloves garlic, chopped
- 1 pound (450g) ground beef
- ½ cup green and red bell pepper, chopped
- 1 cup tomato sauce
- 1 cup milk
- 2 eggs, beaten
- 1 teaspoon ground cumin
- ¼ teaspoon ground cinnamon
- ½ cup parsley, chopped
- 1 teaspoon salt

Method:

- Preheat oven to 350deg. F. (180 deg. C)
- In the meantime, in a greased nonstick pan, add 1/3 of the potatoes.
- Cook for 3 minutes on each side.
- Transfer to a bowl and repeat with remaining potatoes.
- In a greased nonstick pan, add garlic, onion and beef and cook for 3 minutes.
- Add bell peppers, parsley and cinnamon and cook for another 10 minutes.
- In a greased baking dish, spread ½ of the potatoes.
- Top with a layer of beef and another layer of the remaining potatoes.
- In a bowl, whisk eggs and milk.
- Pour over potato mixture.
- Cook in the oven for 30 minutes until golden and firm.
- Allow to cool for 10 minutes before serving.

Nutritional facts:

Serves: 6
Calories: 309 Cal
Fat: 7.4 g
Carbohydrate: 30.7 g
Fiber: 4.9g
Sugar: 6.3 g
Protein: 29.6 g

Picadillo soft taco

Ingredients:

- ½ cup onions, chopped
- 2 teaspoons garlic, chopped
- 1 pound (400 g) grounded turkey breast
- ¼ cup raisin
- 1 teaspoon ground cinnamon
- 1 teaspoon ground cumin
- 14.5 oz. (400 g) canned tomato, diced and un-drained
- 1 avocado, peeled and diced
- 2 tablespoons silvered almonds
- 2 tablespoons fresh cilantro, chopped
- ¾ teaspoon salt
- 8 corn tortillas (6 inch)

Method:

- In a nonstick pan, over medium heat, add garlic, onion and turkey.
- Stir for 4 minutes until turkey is cooked.
- Add raisins, salt, cinnamon, cumin and tomatoes and stir from time to time.
- Simmer for 6 minutes.
- Warm tortillas and add 2/3 cup turkey mixture.
- Add a tablespoon of avocado.
- Sprinkle with some almonds, and cilantro and fold.
- Repeat the process with the other servings.

Nutritional facts:

Serves: 4
Calories: 382 Cal
Fat: 13.0 g
Carbohydrate: 39.9 g
Fiber: 8.8 g
Sugar: 9.4g
Protein: 30.5 g

Baked falafel

Ingredients:

Falafel patties

- 1 clove garlic, minced
- 1 onion, chopped
- ¼ teaspoon cayenne pepper
- 2 tablespoons cilantro, minced
- 1 tablespoon curry powder
- 1 tablespoon parsley, chopped
- 1 tablespoon olive oil
- 2-15 oz. (60g) cans of chickpeas, drained and rinsed
- 1 ½ tablespoons whole wheat flour (or all purpose)
- 2 teaspoons baking powder
- ½ teaspoon salt (optional)
- ½ teaspoon ground black pepper
- 1 tablespoon sesame seeds
- Cooking spray

Sauce

- 1 cup non-fat Greek yoghurt
- ¼ cup tahini
- 1 tablespoon garlic, minced
- 1 tablespoon parsley, minced

Sandwich

- 4 whole wheat pita pockets, cut in half
- 2 tomatoes, sliced (8 slices each)
- ½ onion, thinly sliced

Method:

- Pre-heat oven at 450 deg. F (230 deg. C)
- In a food processor, blend onion, curry powder, cilantro, cayenne pepper, garlic, olive oil and parsley forming a paste.
- Pour chickpeas and chop, ensure that they are still chunky.
- Put salt, pepper and baking soda and blend.
- Place mixture in the refrigerator for 15-20 minutes.
- In the meantime, in a bowl, add tahini, garlic, parsley and yoghurt and mix well.

- Refrigerate until ready to serve.
- Remove falafel mixture from refrigerator and form into balls (approximately 2 tablespoon of mixture each).
- Make 16 falafel balls.
- In a baking tray, lined with baking paper, place the falafel balls.
- Add cooking spray to the balls and dust with sesame seeds.
- Bake falafel balls for 15 minutes on the bottom rack.
- Reduce heat to 350 deg. F (180 deg. C) and continue baking for 15 minutes on the top rack.
- Serve 2 falafel balls on the ½ pita bread.
- Add 2 slices of tomatoes and few slices of onion.
- Drizzle with 2 tablespoons of the sauce.

Nutritional facts:

Serves: 8
Calories: 285 Cal
Fat: 9 g
Carbohydrate: 42 g
Fiber: 9 g
Sugar: 7 g
Protein: 14 g

DESSERTS RECIPES

Blueberry torte dessert

Ingredients:

- 3 eggs, yolk and white separated
- 1 tablespoon sugar
- 1/3 cup ground almonds
- 2 ½ cups fresh blueberries
- 1 teaspoon cornstarch
- ½ cup whipped cream
- 1 teaspoon sugar substitute
- ½ cup organic vanilla yoghurt

Method:

- In a bowl, add sugar and egg yolks and whisk until light.
- Pour almonds.
- In another bowl, add egg whites and beat until firm.
- Fold the egg whites carefully into the egg yolk mixture.
- Pre-heat oven at 350 deg. F (180 deg. C).
- In a lined baking tray with baking paper, add egg mixture and cook for 12-15 minutes.
- Allow to cool outside the oven and cut into 6 squares.
- In the meantime, in a blender, add ½ cup blueberries and puree.
- In a bowl, add cornstarch and cream and mix.
- In a pan, over low heat, add blueberry puree, 2 cups of blueberries and cream mixture.
- Cook for 5 minutes until thickened.
- Add sugar and stir.
- In a serving dish, add blueberry sauce, squares and another layer of blueberry sauce.
- Serve with a spoon of yoghurt.

Nutritional facts:

Serves: 6
Calories: 148 Cal
Fat: 8.1 g
Carbohydrate: 15.3 g
Fiber: 2.1 g
Sugar: 8.4g
Protein: 5.5 g

Angel pecan cupcakes

Ingredients:

- 2 eggs, yolk and whites separated
- ¼ cup hot water
- 1 teaspoon vanilla extract
- ¾ cup fructose
- 1/8 teaspoon salt
- ½ cup cake flour
- ¾ teaspoon low salt baking powder
- ½ cup pecans, chopped

Method:

- Pre-heat oven at 325 deg. F (165 deg. C)
- In a bowl, add egg yolks, vanilla extract and water and mix until light and thickened.
- Add ½ cup fructose and mix slowly. Set aside.
- In another bowl, add egg whites and mix.
- Add salt and continue mixing until partially firm.
- Pour the remaining fructose to the egg white mixture.
- Continue beating until firm.
- Fold 1/3 of egg whites into yolk mixture.
- Strain flour and baking powder over egg mixture.
- Add remaining whites and pecans and gradually blend.
- In a muffin tray, lined with paper liners or slightly greased, pour batter equally distributed.
- Bake for 20 minutes or until cooked.

Nutritional facts:

Serves: 12
Calories: 93 Cal
Fat: 1.6 g
Carbohydrate: 19.0 g
Fiber: 0.0 g
Sugar: 5.3 g
Protein: 1.6 g

Chocolate cake

Ingredients:

- 2 cups self raising flour
- 1/3 cup cocoa powder
- ½ teaspoon bicarbonate soda
- 2/3 cup sugar
- 2 eggs
- ¼ cup canola oil
- 1 cup skim milk
- 7 oz. (200g) low fat vanilla yoghurt
- 1 teaspoon vanilla essence
- 5 medium strawberries, hulled and sliced
- 1 tablespoon icing sugar

Method:

- Pre-heat oven at 320 deg. F (160 deg. C)
- In a bowl, sift flour, bicarbonate soda and cocoa.
- Add sugar and mix.
- In another bowl, add eggs, yoghurt, milk, oil and vanilla essence and mix.
- Transfer egg mixture in the center of the dry mixture and combine.
- In greased cake mold, add mixture.
- Bake for 50 minutes or until cooked.
- Remove from oven and allow resting for 5 minutes.
- Turn cake over wire rack to cool.
- Sprinkle icing sugar and add strawberries to decorate.

Nutritional facts:

Serves: 12
Calories: 203 Cal
Fat: 6.1 g
Carbohydrate: 33.2 g
Fiber: 1.4 g
Sugar: 13.1g
Protein: 5.1 g

Banana chocolate parfaits

Ingredients:

- 1 cup plain low fat yoghurt
- 1, 0.8 oz. (22g) box sugar free chocolate pudding mix
- 2 bananas, cut into 4 pieces
- 1 teaspoon fresh lemon juice
- ¼ cup reduced fat frozen dairy whipping topping
- Unsweetened cocoa powder
- 1 tablespoon walnuts, chopped (optional)
- 4 fresh raspberries (or any other berries)

Method:

- Prepare pudding according to instructions on the packet.
- Mix pudding with yoghurt.
- Dust bananas with lemon juice.
- In 4 dessert glasses, add banana quarters, ¼ pudding mix and whipping cream in each.
- Sift cocoa powder on each serve.
- Sprinkle with walnuts.
- Add berries and serve.

Nutritional facts:

Serves: 4
Calories: 138 Cal
Fat: 3 g
Carbohydrate: 25 g
Fiber: 2 g
Sugar: 9.7 g
Protein: 4 g

Baked cinnamon stuffed apples

Ingredients:

- 4 large apples, cored
- ½ lemon juice
- ¼ cup plus 2 tablespoons brown sugar blend
- ¼ cup oatmeal
- 1 teaspoon cinnamon
- 2 tablespoons fat free margarine
- ¼ cup pecans, chopped

Method:

- Pre-heat oven at 425 deg. F (220 deg. C)
- In a bowl, add sugar, oatmeal, cinnamon, pecans and margarine and mix.
- Sprinkle apples with lemon juice.
- Fill each apple with ¼ of the mixture.
- In a greased baking tray, place apples.
- Bake for 25-30 minutes.
- Serve.

Nutritional facts:

Serves: 4
Calories: 224 Cal
Fat: 3.1 g
Carbohydrate: 47.5 g
Fiber: 6.6 g
Sugar: 35.4g
Protein: 1 g

Mini pumpkins tarts

Ingredients:

- 30 mini-Nilla wafer cookies
- 8 oz. (225g) light cream cheese, softened
- 1 egg
- ¼ cup light sour cream
- ¼ cup Splenda sugar blend
- ½ teaspoon vanilla
- ¾ cup canned pure pumpkin
- ½ cinnamon
- Pinch nutmeg
- 30 baking cups

Method:

- Pre-heat oven at 350 deg. F (180 deg. C).
- In a bowl, add cream cheese, egg, sour cream, vanilla, sugar, pure pumpkin, cinnamon and nutmeg and mix until smooth (use electric mixer).
- In a mini-muffin pan, lined with baking cups, place wafers (one on each cup).
- Add the cheese mixture equally in each cup.
- Put pan in the oven.
- Bake for 30 minutes or until cooked.
- Allow cooling and serve.

Nutritional facts:

Serves: 30
Calories: 40 Cal
Fat: 2.5 g
Carbohydrate: 4 g
Fiber: 0 g
Sugar: 3 g
Protein: 1 g

Frozen strawberries fruit pops

Ingredients:

- 12 strawberries
- 12 cake pop sticks
- ½ cup nonfat blueberry Greek yoghurt
- ¼ cup pecans, chopped

Method:

- Carefully stick a pop stick into the cap or "hull" of each strawberry, without braking.
- Immerse each strawberry in the yoghurt (thinly coated).
- Dust each strawberry with a teaspoon of pecan.
- In a baking sheet, place each strawberry pop.
- Put in the freezer for 1-2 hours until yoghurt is solid.
- Remove and serve.

Nutritional facts:

Serves: 12
Calories: 55 Cal
Fat: 3.5 g
Carbohydrate: 5 g
Fiber: 1 g
Sugar: 3 g
Protein: 2 g

DRINK RECIPES

Celery Smoothie

Ingredients:

- 2 stalks celery, chopped
- 1 small banana, peeled and sliced
- ½ cup baby spinach
- 1 cup plain yogurt
- ½ cup fat free milk

Method:

- Place the celery, banana, spinach, yogurt and milk into the food processor.
- Blend until smooth.
- Pour into glasses and serve chilled.

Nutritional facts:

Serves: 4
Calories: 159 Cal
Fat: 1.6 g
Carbohydrates: 23.9 g
Fibers: 1.9 g
Sugars: 18.0 g
Proteins: 9.8 g

Blueberry Orange Frappe

Ingredients:

- 2 oranges, peeled and sectioned
- 3 teaspoons orange zest
- 2 cups skimmed milk
- 1¼ cups frozen blueberries

Method:

- Add oranges, orange zest, skimmed milk and blueberries in a food processor and blend until smooth.
- Pour into glasses and serve.

Nutritional facts:

Serves: 4
Calories: 109 Cal
Fats: 0.3g
Carbohydrates: 23.3g
Fiber: 3.5g
Sugars: 13.1g
Protein: 4.6g

Cranberry Milkshake

Ingredients:

- 1½ bananas, peeled and sliced
- 1½ cups fresh cranberries
- 1 cup skimmed milk
- ½ cup ice

Method:

- Add bananas, cranberries, milk and ice into a food processor and blend until smooth.
- Pour into glasses and serve.

Nutritional facts:

Serves: 3
Calories: 100 Cal
Fats: 0.1g
Carbohydrates: 23.0g
Fiber: 3.9g
Sugars: 8.9g
Protein: 3.0g

Acai Banana Smoothie

Ingredients:

- 2 (7 oz. each) frozen acai packages
- 2 medium bananas, peeled and sliced
- 1 teaspoon honey
- 1 teaspoon vanilla extract
- ½ cup ice

Method:

- Add acai, bananas, honey, vanilla and ice in a food processor and blend until smooth.
- Pour into glasses and serve.

Nutritional facts:

Serves: 2
Calories: 122 Cal
Fats: 0.0g
Carbohydrates: 30.0g
Fiber: 3.5g
Sugars: 17.2g
Protein: 1.2g

Mango and Pineapple Frappe

Ingredients:

- 1 cup frozen mango chunks
- ½ cup pineapple cubes
- ¼ cup passion fruit pulp
- 6 ice cubes

Method:

- Place mango chunks, pineapple cubes, passion fruit pulp and ice cubes into the food processor.
- Blend until smooth.
- Pour into glasses and serve.

Nutritional facts:

Serves: 2
Calories: 49
Fat: 0.3g
Carbohydrates: 12.3g
Fibers: 3.6g
Sugars: 7.4g
Protein:

Kale and Apple Smoothie

Ingredients:

- 2 cups kale
- 2 green apples, peeled, cored and diced
- ¼ cup almonds, chopped
- ¼ cup fresh apple juice
- 6 ice cubes

Method:

- In a food processor, add kale, apples, almonds, apple juice and ice.
- Blend until smooth.
- Pour into glasses and serve.

Nutritional facts:

Serves: 2
Calories: 211 Cal
Fat: 6.0g
Carbohydrates: 38.3g
Fibers: 6.9g
Sugars: 22.8g
Proteins: 4.5g

Sugar free hot chocolate

Ingredients:

- 1 package of non-fat dry milk
- 8 tablespoons Hershey's cocoa
- 8-10 tablespoons Stevia (in the raw)
- ½ teaspoon ground cinnamon (optional)

Method:

- In a bowl, add dry milk, cocoa, cinnamon and stevia and mix.
- Add mixture into an air-tight container.
- In a mug, add 1/3- ½ cup of mixture and hot water.
- Serve with a drop of vanilla (optional).

Nutritional facts:

Serves: 4
Calories: 134 Cal
Fat: 1.7 g
Carbohydrates: 21.7 g
Fibers: 3.7 g
Sugars: 15.8 g
Proteins: 13.0 g

REFERENCE

www.idf.org

www.diabetes.org

www.childrenwithdiabetes.com

www.webmd.com/diabetes

www.kidshealth.org

www.mayoclinic.org

www.betterhealth.vig.gov.au

www.diabtesaustralia.com.au

www.diabetesvic.org.au/living-with-diabtes

CONCLUSION

Diabetes Type 1 is an autoimmune condition that destroys the insulin producing cells. A child with diabetes needs to strengthen the immune system by removing the foods that might activate an immune reaction and incorporating nutritional foods. Your child might also benefit from eating low GI foods, such as: oats, porridge, muesli, whole meal, nuts, seeds, potatoes, pasta, legumes, long grain rice, fruits and vegetables.

The key to your child's health and happiness is monitoring the blood sugar, having a diabetes plan specifically designed for the child and the support of family, friends and a health care team.

Check the other books by

Elizabeth Ambrose.

Go to **"for the lovers of coffee"** at **amazon.com** or amazon and your country code and order your copy. Or click the picture.

Go to **"The best Smoothies, Milkshakes and Frappes"** at **amazon.com** or Amazon and your country code and order your copy. Or click the picture.

Go to **"Berry good diet, the perfect Superfood diet"** at **amazon.com** or Amazon and your country code and order your copy. Or click the picture.

Go to **"Argentinian Paleo Cookbook"** at **amazon.com** or Amazon and your country code and order your copy. Or click the picture.

Go to **"Grilling and barbecuing your way through summer"** at **amazon.com** or Amazon and your country code and order your copy. Or click the picture

Thank you

Thank you for reading this book.

I hope you enjoyed it!

If you liked this book I would appreciate if you could take a minute and leave a review with your feedback.

Just go to **Amazon.com**

Look for **"Raising happy and healthy children with diabetes"**

A guide for parents and delicious recipes for your child and the whole family.

by Elizabeth Ambrose

and

Click on "write a customer review"

Thank you!

Printed in Poland
by Amazon Fulfillment
Poland Sp. z o.o., Wrocław